D1367322

FRANK 207

Also by Raphael Rudnik:

A Lesson From The Cyclops and other poems

In The Heart Or Our City

FRANK 207

poems by Raphael Rudnik

Ohio University Press
Athens, Ohio

Library of Congress Cataloguing in Publication Data

Rudnik, Raphael.
  Frank 207, and other poems.

    I. Title.
PS3568.U35F7   811'.54   81-16914
ISBN 0-8214-0634-5   AACR2
ISBN 0-8214-0635-3 (pbk.)

For M

Grateful acknowledgement is made to the editors of the following publications in which these poems first appeared:

CAPstan Anthology: *Let It Come Down.*
Maatstaf (Holland): *The Boston Strangler, Mythology,* and *"He—Belonged-To . . ?"*
Moondance: *For Jules Laforgue.*
The Nation: *End, Lachiman Gurung Gurka From Nepal, In Highgate Cemetery London, To A Painter, Ghosts* and *The Window Cleaner.*
Open Places: *Frank 207, Copy-Boy* and *Amsterdam Street-Scene 1972.*
Plainsong: *The Mountains in Holland.*
Poetry: *You Are Something Shining, In A Garden, The Devils, Dream, Now That Your Body* and *Seasons and Stars.*
Present Tense: *The Children.*
Shenandoah: *That Sunny Day You Walked The Master Home.*

Amsterdam Street-Scene, 1972 appeared in the Puschart Prize V Anthology.

Thanks are also given to the New York State Council on the Arts for a CAPS award.

CONTENTS

ONE

YOU ARE SOMETHING SHINING

You are something shining not nothing mirroring
madness like an island of inviolable flowers
burning up in deep-colored streams to tops
of murdered mountains whose immense and actual
appearances look down upon a bright confusion

of suspicion that there are flowers
which keep coming in gliding on the
glassy undersides of waves arriving
with a wild kissing laugh and sad white rush
while the endlessly suiciding sea does not care.

FRANK 207

*The Mayor announced today the formation of a new City anti-
graffiti task force to develop tough new programs to stop the effects
of the graffiti epidemic. Directing a wide group of City officials to
begin a new, comprehensive task force effort: "New measures are
needed on all fronts to halt this assault on our senses, to prevent and
remove these marks that constantly appear, disfiguring scrawlings
ablaze on monuments and buildings, covering comfort stations,
benches, handball-walls, signs, entirely changing fences and facades,
abusing rocks, and even trees are targets—but especially buses and
subways—all our public places marred with unsightliness and un-
pleasantness, ugly, obscene blobs, names, or nicknames, and num-
bers, pointless, sprayed on by vandals. The whole city suffers greatly
from this evil."*

*The task force, directed by the Mayor's Chief of Staff Steven L.
Isenburg, will include high-ranking representatives designated by the
following heads of agencies and offices:*

> *Corporation Counsel Norman Redlich*
> *Environmental Protection Administrator Jerome Kretchner*
> *Municipal Service Administrator Milton Musicus*
> *Police Commissioner Patrick V. Murphy*
> *Transportation Administrator Constantine Sidamon-Eristoff*
> *Director of the Criminal Justice Coordinating Council*
> *Henry Ruth*
> *Acting Director of the Office of Neighborhood Government*
> *John Mudd*

*   *

The letters of it came, the letters of
his name, he loved his name—coming out of
the hollow, hissing can onto smiling
subway tiles. It would stay bright not grow old
like a dream. Lemurlike, the boy waited.
As light dawned on the rails, the big boxes
full of people and light came in, opened.
But they all walked by, the sentinels of

4

themselves, hurrying out, seeing nothing.
Still gleaming, bursting red sausages
ended up in the little slipper-kicks of
crude serifs, and once—no, twice where his
hand had wavered they wore nightmare-hats,
on the number of the street where he lived.
The wall had eyes now, in which there was shut
the emotion of a multitude. Then,
a moment of momentous silence
as he got on the next train dreaming that
Coco and Phil threw someone through a plate-glass
window and after he went down into
the store inside I bet he wished he had
no head and when he got up staggered out and
wrote his name red all over the sidewalk
but no one could read it he wrote so bad.
Haw. The train came out of the underworld.
Hurtling in an empty silent space, he found
a cracked cobweb in glass around a hole in
the sky. Placed his rigid red net there, thinking
now John Q. Citizen has got a new task
force just for us and one of them so help me
his name is Mudd so I guess we must spray
him too up the ass we read the papers.

LET IT COME DOWN

The woman did not stop seeing that
Black bracelet of flies stuck on her leg.
And in her face, pain was an idea. *Hers.*
She was the one leaving coins of blood
Falling glittering into cement sea.

THE WINDOW CLEANER

The window cleaner is on the wide, dirty ledge
again, laughingly
asking my wife to give him a hand—
pull him in, or pull her out?
It's like a question in a dream.

He swaggered up that frightening ladder,
smiling at the sky
as if he would be feeling even better
walking on heaven's ceiling—
hardmouthed, stupid, cruel, and unnecessary.

At the sight of a pretty woman,
he has those permanently wounded eyes
which are more troubling than one can see or say.
He starts to work, I get a severed-head effect, wobbling
and blurring as he washes the worsening atmosphere away. Then

the tensed, hurdling muscle of his whole body leans backward,
from the ladder; hands holding pail and blade, the arms go out
like a balcony, embracing air; feet, balancing, step down;
and, out of his face—
pours the brightness which is vigor which is beauty in a man.

GHOSTS

That man crawled halfway up our bed
In sleep, after he knocked on the door,
At night in a little house by the sea,
Telling us he had seen ghosts on the road
That came once to our door—crying he, we
Would die—terrifying, drifting pallor
To the bed he dropped his hollow load
Like the sea falling big, cold, dead . . .

NOW THAT YOUR BODY

Now that your body
Like a golden rose
Has been touched and entered more
Than I suppose
Is good for it, or me—

The petals rush and close,
On their own mystery—
And the face floating free
In light knows
As before.

END

Earth spinning in toy-like complacency, stopped. Bright ball
Hit by a dark tangent. Hurtling off, everything—all
Gleams striking into, shuddering through space. Things,
And natural things, the animals, man and woman, time. Grandeur
Of splendor of disaster shaken free
From gravity. This was the end we all had to fear. Blind,
Rehearsing catastrophies in the cave of the mind.
Discovering silken light in our towers of flesh. Falling
Radiant and singular, attending each other,
Like white ghosts of the sea breaking, making land a body.

BEAUTY

Rich rare redness of the hurt fox, then pride
(So great a bounty is set on his hide) cleverly fears.
Frail architecture of bone performing inside
Thousand-eyed feathers when peacocks preen and stalk and strut.
Beauty desires (any strange, unaccustomed grace)

Such things, and her own—amazed, made fire-clear—
Face
Rising, shattering the
Shut
Brute blue beast sea.

TREES BEARING CLOUDS

white nubs stare   through the green labyrinth   of blossoms so that
moving limbs of smoke   wildly fed by the fire   they will not forget past pains

THE DEVILS

The devils felt goodness when they were angels,
But did not understand what to do
As the terrible annunciations rang
Proclaiming that everything was love.

So gave back to the vault of heaven, desire—
And becoming, then trying to be, power—

They fell, embracing fire with wings of fire.

THAT SUNNY DAY, YOU WALKED
THE MASTER HOME

1.

In an anti-symbolical little cell
Near Rome, you spoke to the edge of force still
In him, facing you—*George Santayana.* All
Your youth and gaiety, ambassadorial,

Introduced itself, breaking the humdrum,
Told him you had read *The Sense of Beauty*,
And of your army job, rationing in Rome.
That mustered light into sick eyes, hungry.

2.

You thought that he was dying, and hiding
From the fact of his life, talking to you.
The greatest crime is to be confiding
Without feeling, passion, or thought—thought you.

So you decided to give him the best,
Of Thomas Martin, Romantic, U.S.A.:
"Better to be vile than vile-esteemed—best
To teach you philosophers how to lay!"

3.

You were a poet and a criminal both.
So, could rail against black-market connections,
And *real* prices, with such heaven-storming wrath
He had to laugh and like it. But, erections

Were your real subject: "The clip and suck, art
Of sex, in the rhythm of *The Sonnets*, more
Show Shakespeare's heart hard ... than his other part."
And you could be a blue and bloody bore:

4.

"'My thing is so big, I don't know what to do'
Started my sonnet of today. *Rhyme*
And Reason? Booze and Shit on You—
The title. Writing it, cost me a good time

With that golden-haired fat-woman whore,
Who insisted her pay should be being
Squired around the army-base, *'visa d'amore,'*
By big-shot me. The whole army seeing

Her equipment. A goddess-tourist.
I had her, then paid—said I would not do it.
Sweating her out in the sonnet. Masochist
Petrarch was wired-up in her gold hair. *Screw it—*

'Gold shit' was what I metaphored her to . . .
But then, 'she carried a bomb between her legs;
Flame puffed, pulled them apart, moaning O,
I saw her bloody shoes, standing alone . . . her dregs.'"

5.

You talked like a talking penis—(and he
Looked a little like one, a little one,
That purple-veined bullet-headed mystery
And misery of a face, shining sun).

6.

Old philosopher, nodding his hurt head.
Your style of thinking was Eclectic Bad,
But you were the truth of what you said, he said.
Pure proof that art was neither good nor bad,

But merely a "homesickness for the world"—
That sort of thing he had. Old man, dying?
The day was a bright, spinal ball curled
On his bed. And . . . the echo, like crying.

7.

Translating, Lodovico Della Vernaccia's
Sonnet *He Exhorts The State to Vigilance*
Like this: "O souls, loving awe and brilliance,
You who would kill or die for Americas

Unknown, undiscovered archipelagos
Of power—all you who have not yet made
Peace with your enemies, now smell here those
Rotten hearts. Oh, listen sharp as blades!

There are those who do not want to be good
Citizens. Poor-mouthed vile sullen upstarts,
Mindless mouths chewing their own meat for food,
Issuing forth turd-words of truth, fierce farts

Of eloquence. All—all against the State!
Act now, or be bitten by this mad many.
Use knife, gun, hands, before it is too late.
Power powerless, cannot kill any!"

8.

Santayana: "More of Martin there, than
The model." *You*: "I made that Italian
Troubadour crazy on politics, as if...
He was a C.I.A. weird with the syph!"—

—"But, in his poem where spirit hardens
Into a kind of atavistic badness,
There is a second poem—with rich gardens
Of feeling, defended by great gladness."—

—"I meant to show that man survives himself."
—"There is such a thing as the human spirit..."
—"Centuries kept Vernaccia on the shelf,
Just because he had no poetic merit..."

9.

You filled his little corner with it all,
Until he turned his face toward the wall.

Then yellow light fluttering near his mouth,
Spoke your crowning ornament: *"You speak the truth."*

10.

You loved the old man, fed him your gold. "You
Utter, utter—amiable cow!" he thrilled,
Breaking off a piece of chocolate. You
Were just about to go. His table, filled.

"You've given me too many rations, I beg—
Give them—*to God*, or Marshall Tito. That
Man can be trusted . . . I know, because his dog
Accompanies him on trips of State."

11.

But suddenly there was No One in his bed.
"For hym deth grippeth right hard by the hed"
A voice snarled in you, and then asked the reason
Black stuff was near the bed, called it "treason."

12.

"This sunny day, I walked The Master home"
Was what you wrote that night, in a poem.
All death is suspect of a martyrdom
The current of life can never become.

in memory of Thomas K. Martin

COUNTERMAN

His rag went a-washing in stiff, short arcs that showed
Something else was going on, the surface before me bright, wet,
A mirror for his upside-down face ablaze with pleasure at . . .
The O, lovely flexible presence then bestowed.

Big, gleaming. Air seemed to heave her rose-petal smooth roundedness
To parturition, an ordureous sweatiness.
Flame-colored hair a shocking cloud, curdling the mind.
The tip of a towel dipped into water rubbed along blind.

COPY-BOY

Languidly seething uncontrollable anxiety that he
cannot create an atmosphere of low menace enough
with the cruelty of indifference—then the tight, faded sex-pouched
    jeans going
into a series of death-throe bumps and grinds and twitches
that tallish torso-twisted-back in the lumberjack shirt seemed un-
conscious of, his face, almost hidden by beard-hair and hair, black
    woolly tufts
too long to stand up, slack flags flaunting youth—but beautiful
    (which means
all the animals which came together in him made a harmony
which hid them all).
                The copy-boy for *The American Banker* daily
    stood over
the Dow-Jones tickertape, lifting the scrolls, reading their signs.
(Fallen angels must find something when they fall, become someone
somewhere, somehow. Not only falling, but slammed into earth, this
    one—
has odd blue eyes, right one seems set a bit higher than the left—
looks deeply hurt.) Says nothing, keeps stroking his hair, all
    nerved-up.

Taut, attent fingers atop the machine made mountains of their
    knuckles, fallen flat,
his hands worked out in front of him, twisting wrists, manipulating
    thumb-knobs (as if
they were an instrument instructing his heart it could stop carry-
    ing its knowledge
one moment to the next).
                He, (or his grandfather rocking alone
    with him
on some mid-Western porch in the dark years ago) seemed to consider
hurdling it, *be a boy again!*—but an end-of-the-day dimness darkened
bright-blue clear-eyed discs and instead, a fast tip of tongue

tasted the mouth that foolishly smiled and then said:
"These God-damned Jews!"

                And, *"it figures,"* when I told him I
was one—
(a comic angel, mindlessly judging his own odyssey)...

THE BOSTON STRANGLER

A revolving ball of fire, in front of a black mirror.

Told to manipulate her limbs every day, even though
She cried, played her flat on her back and evenly and slow
Opened, closed half-sunk thighs like bellows. He had to hurt her
To help her, she was his child loved very deeply, not dead.
Silver-shadowed hair, twenty-five cents yellow ribbon bow.

All this talk about intercourse and strangling(s) with strangers—
He never struck at anyone, only images, no—
Attractiveness had nothing to do with it—napkins red,
Cigarettes, and stockings to tie around the neck—it all *Oh*,
Left him cold now. Locked in a dull fierce gaze somewhere.

                                                    "But, who
Sent you?"..."OK. The Superintendent. Says something's wrong here.
Your bathroom, got to check it out"..."I don't see no leak, *where?*"
"Lie down"..."I can't do nothing, my doctor told me: 'No!'" *"There!"*
"...I gave him to eat, and in the summer I sent his bed
To the country. *Immer!* I don't feel well."—
                                    Deep, deep, deeper.
A ball of fire revolving in front of a black mirror.

MYTHOLOGY

A filthy, cloudy hallway.
> Sat behind two orange-crates, a door flat
> atop them.
Lit a thick candle on it—light-hollow, black rim—face like a girl
who had just seen
A gorgon—*or a gorgon!* A glimmering white porcelain dog above
each box,
Hid life like a bone. (One with wise, sad paranoic eyes, baroque
plumed tail, chest great
As a lion's thigh; the other's eyes pale blue painted so somehow
they looked tilted
Back in his head, a hell-hound's.) The candle's flame green as grass,
wriggling (shifting shadows
On her moonous, mirroring face changed it from mad to glad to sad
fast) then went still
(A cat's eye, a little seeing leaf, whitish-yellow again). You could
see her stare,
Simply guarding the shameful secret (the exact nature of despair is
to be

Unaware of it) her emptiness, so full of one force or feeling—all awe
And brilliance at time's agonizing nostalgia—she could not be
part of
Her own life.
> The mind knows only what lies near the heart.
> > Filled
> with color-kissing joy
Of light, eyes jerked around like nervous dice, hunting the happy
animal light;—now
It was a burning flower she followed, each change a part of her
destination . . .

The candle dims, she's tipping it (her hands' wrinkles red as cuts
somehow attractive)
Drips wax on finger-ends, the first two (the rest tensed, clawed)
sliding together smoothly

In an imaginary money-sign.
                                Burns back up; grins, lit from beneath.
        Death's-head.

The gods are doomed, and the end is death, a greater than all . . .
        receiving wax-fragments,
The tears of her grief . . .
                        She's *Diana*,—of course! But as she would
        be now, escaping her
Mythology.

                        A madwoman on Welfare who asked me as I passed—(I
        grabbed walls,
One leg refused to move, asleep from sitting on the stairs so long
        scrunched up spying
On her round a corner, it felt as if it was full of seltzer, almost
        knocked her
Hound over)——asked, did I want to contribute to *Dogs for
        Rockefeller?* He was
The one who would say who did what to whom and where and when.

TWO

TRYING OUT THE DREAM

a fragment

At first it was so fast that all things seemed to hide it just by being there. Then yellow shining free of the sky, like another sun.

Our tricky black dome bounced hilariously, slowed to the silent black car of a beetle, stopped. A white wood bridge gave a blank stare. Air was concussion. Grass lay down in long smooth swirls, as if cows had slept on it.

Postic pointed his cigar—a receding orange eye, stroked by smoke—at the sky.

Rays, or arms of fire were shooting out of that second sun, slowly falling, straggling red streamers of living matter, loosely united, but often allowed great freedom being unattached—shifting, vaulting, dropping through each other; or curbing, spurring, self-isolating themselves as they fell—you could see it was not weight pulled them down . . . into that great pool of glittering shadow wobbling on the horizon, where the city had been.

Hisses bloomed into words. The driver, using the wind to shake his hat free of dust—: "Looks like we miss it." "The race?" "No, the bomb—it's going to have lunch in the city." Postic then: "So what are we doing here—*sight*-seeing?"

Postic opened Clocker Bob's big green racing-sheet; and atop that wall which hid him from the world, his gay, bedizened headband held grey hair stiff as a whiskbroom and the famous, foolish lucky-mystery feather (the one he let fall before every big bet)—smiling up to light, or sitting in darkness as we rode through bomb-brightened zones. Below, shiny-electric purple pants filled pneumatic, spinach-green socks stuffed into deadly-pointed black shoes whose golden eyeholes gulped blood-colored strings—and all that seemed to strut standing still.

Irony at work everywhere; rounding his arm as his hand turned the pages, blind partition behind partition in front of his face, and in a loud stage-whisper voice, Postic menstruating all over the expert who predicted an easy race for JUMPING STEEL, (a big, rugged colt who had beaten the great CANNONADE and the famed JUDGER) because he was "quick and shifty, always came out of the gate on his toes, ran gamely, and never had been out of the money."—

The car hiccoughed a lurching bounce; lifting the paper enough to show Postic's baby-blue T-shirt full of plump pink hearts afloat, washed-out yet emphatic as hearts heralding love in a cartoon. Hunched under his hunches, he's crouched forward—so that that stomach swaying inside the great loosened sack of shirt . . . mutated those hearts into strangely swollen stars—for a moment, before the green pages came down again, and were turned to, *ah!* The histories of the horses, and the names. Their names looked fabulous in that afternoon: KOKO-DOZO, MOONSHOT, JILLION BARRELS, JUMPING STEEL, AMALIA, REVERBERATOR, AGO, ICY DAY, BEE BEE BEE, PERSIAN CLAW, WHO IS COUGHING?, CLAPHAM JUNCTION, and SILVER SHIP.

A roaring gutteral out of the sky, as we passed the shrunken grey city of a cemetery. Humpy (the driver) slowed to motoring royalty. Frankensteining a stalled, menacing dull whine, his foot wedged against the gas—.

Wind came into the car, seizing breath, pulled the rattling paper free from its reader, our leader . . . ;—flapping onto our legs, it fell to the floor, stopped, puffed, shrank . . . in an invisible, fatal rain. Postic's gasping breathlessly mechanized (a sick man who crawled to the track all his life) oracular grunts, that *this is not that spinning wind which broke down the city*, but a psychic blast (he's not a form-follower, knows nothing of past performances, work-outs, or jockeys, or about horses, though he squints and smiles and frowns in simian wonder over the charts, Postic's really looking with his original eyes at the dark words and numbers wintering on the page for a tiny clue, to strike with lightning-rightness, tell who will win the race, show the red Adam in him the name *happening*, with some triumphant movement the name cannot express becoming the future event of itself, world into word, in its very letters, or numbers—no, not by making sense of facts and figures, figuring out what horse might suddenly become sudden, or, trying the tried and known favorites brandished by Bob The Clocker and other "expert" profit-prophets,—*no*, it is an inward-soaring, hushed and roused swift motion of the mind entering some never-failing region of . . . well, *he* sees it . . . somehow, warm levers and icy trances, also the spicy smell of death, perhaps, taking him . . . hit by some dark tangent, those ant-holes of language in the living and dead, the alive green wood—breaking, opening—bronzed by the blood of time!)

Whoa!

What a wild thing, to try to ride his rhetorical horse! Better, an example—once SWORD DANCER's second "r" had a sharp, broken little serif kicking out ahead of itself, so that the blade showed P. the name itself was cutting into time, doing its dance, being itself, as if it would be seen so when it won and was a result—and sure enough the horse came through, paying $34.60 that day before anyone (else) knew it was a great one! Say it simply: Postic (how rightly named) believes past present and future are the same thing happening together somewhere, somehow . . . some/time. Get my meaning? (How can the future become diminished, if it is not yet here? Or how the past, which is disappeared, become increased—and the present, always continuing with no space, although it passes away in a moment?) The motion and variety we live-by by ignorance, keeps extinguishing the mind—expecting the future, keeping consideration of it going into the present, and conveying these over, over again and again, so as to become past, memory. *But*, the future has already happened, too! We just don't know it any more than fish the shore they swim by. Time's agonizing nostalgia . . . It has a whip being snapped, waved over us, never really touching till the end of the race; makes man move because he doesn't like knowing, *not* knowing. He just lolly-gags around time's track with his tongue hanging out of his mouth. A certain loss of dignity in that. But, Postic has a gaudy hook he can poke through the present with the future. A thing beyond asking or thinking, how he does it. He dies a little, falling free from his five senses "through that black declinity, 'I'"—past all distractions which give him "paper-cuts on the brain." All life out, or dark. Going in an invisible arc, into . . . finding the name, inside himself. A commonplace, I know. Such psychic stuff. This may seem to be superficial;

but it is in fact profound. He *wins*! That's the fact. Somehow—he can stand, shifting around just enough on the slender platform of his mind, to make a crazy plank spring up and hit him right in the head with the name of the winning horse! It hurts, but—not him, it seems! He says *"he can taste Time's blood!"* Now, what does that mean? Then (usually, at the last moment before a big race) he drops it, O—I forgot, the feather!

... Back in the car, going out to the track. When he let that "mythic wind" take it. First, plucked it out, *bah* .. (it always looks crooked, tired, as if it had grown through his head.) Between fingertips like great wings on a tiny body which could only be touched, not held. Let it go. *Bright fall.* Writhing as if on fire in the strange light ... You know—, Postic always goes on about the way it falls each time, toppling, floundering, sinking, bowing, drowning, being humiliated (a *feather!*), yielding, gasping, and biting the dust. That downy, undulating nether-feather of his has, *been up there where we could never be, the clouds, the sky!* This time, although "under attack" ... it "changed chance into choice." Making one nervous, tight erratic twirl, then helicoptering straight down, dug a divot like an auger-bit; it stuck point-first into the paper, starchy stuff, doughy-white now, not marvellous ... into the name, whose letters looked darker fresher ... But, *it* didn't do anything! Why, with a short, harsh bark of laughter ... he even seemed to be holding it up in the air for a moment, untouched, with pure ....

Dream-power!

Swiftness and certitude require strength, and Postic has this strength. When he gets that golden, blasting feeling. All contingency and naturalness; the oddness is the naturalness. No stranger than any-thing else. Really. And as I said, he doesn't need to hop and pick about the dung of *Clocker*'s (or the others') racing-history rubbish.. *"Beetles rolling a ball of dung,"* he calls them ... how he hates History! (Though very shards are bright where he has sung its strange and silent song, to *us!*) Strange singer.. These facts, I know: as a sales-man he sold something "self-drilling, self-filling, a core .. made of gold, of course, because it's durable, easily divisible, compact in weight, convenient to handle, consistent in quality, and because it's highly valued apart from its use in dental work." You tell 'em, Postic! Our star salesman of the soul also sold mats, shiny wooden pillars, brightly colored maps of . . ? he blows down his nostrils in amusement when I ask where. . . . It would have to be someplace special I say, and leave it at that. Best of all, once when I was stern and cold, scolding him like a stranger for telling us nothing new or true about himself, he grinned and climbing out of the car near a field that was like a radiant crust of light—gazing at the grain he says: *"I used to sell do-it-yourself face-lifting kits on the phone to beauty-shops in Kansas."* Sure. Yippity-yip. And shin-guards for crickets. —Then, dammit, so be it. We *understand* even if we don't know or believe what P. is talking about; we know what he is and what not. We see him nude, drinking beer.

Postic. ("Oh. Him.") It came back to that every time . . . the moment of the movement (his) is always *"now"*; and everything in the world can do it when he's *"right."* A woman tottering like a colt, heels caught in a crack in the sidewalk, while doing a sexual genuflection to right herself, lavished the raw, flagrant manner of a foolish look on Postic. FOOLISH FILLY won (and paid $10.80). A strange cloud, all light held within it, the only one in the sky, floating into his mind, showed BRIGHT MORNING would win (and it did, paid $28.90). O, and a waiter carrying soup to him with one hand had not one but two thumbs a-floating in it—Humpy the driver had his fun, while those two dumb phallic thumbs there where one should (shouldn't) be got gawks from all the rest of us, he hawked his delicate profile at the waiter, asked what kind of soup it was. Fish-soup. Oh, what's in it? *Fish* . . . . I guess you have to be there. Anyway, the waiter's "tip" to us (to P.)—that HANDS OFF would beat the favored FISH TO DAY was worth $45 even. (I can't tell anymore in this what we bet when we win—all prices given show only what a $2 bet would have won—mustn't Postic says, it's a sin like taking a census.)

So you see, anything in the world can do it for him. A cloud, a cunt, a freak. Oh, and then there's the numbers game! More easy and, more difficult; because he can't get it up in this with anything but pure dream-power; no who what when and where for lightning-rods, making connections with winning program-numbers, post-positions. Postic *did* really dream that once, a long line of winning numbers, daily-doubles, saw five of them clearly: the first race-winner going linked hand-in-hand with the second, hyphenated— Giant, block-seriffed things marching stiff-legged, or monumentally

slithering along on their curves, like a faceless row of kings (there were more, their slender and big heads shadowy, but *there*, moving on). The winning numbers! Great neuters in the realm of cash! But— the only one in the world to know—and he forgot! Postic. Remembered the last pair in the dream-procession only, 3–1. We played it, trying out the dream, and it *won*—it won and paid $131.60. $131.60! We could have followed that dream till it devoured all money . . . .
I asked, P., once, how much money he wanted to win: *"All* money," he said. "So do I," I said. He said doubtfully, "I suppose I could." But, then—It was the *Twin* who did it! Phoned P. that morning and the dream shattered. The numbers broke in his head like yellow clouds with bits of green and brown, as he spoke into their faint, clacking bug of a tape: *". . . pointed yellow leaves, going slowly on grey water, anglers flicking maggots on hooks to wily fish . . Dollars, dollars.—What do I always get? . . . . long antennae, hairy wings, and successive instars, hatched from a much smaller egg dropped without much ceremony upon a stone in a stream bed—"* He talked about insects not numbers;—why did they bug him? *The Twins* hoped something would tumble out of the dark tank of his mind when they broke in on him in the middle of a dream. They had someone put in a fresh reel every day, you could hear the bug click clearly. (Usually all they got was Postic's sweaty sleeplessness when they woke him, or a kind of clear alphabet-soup, he reciting letters floating and knocking around in his brain-pan, or deeper down: all his paranoid tribunals hastily assembled, or unemployed angels and horrors, and time itself—*"You've been down there something where the dark is not"*——or a box of harpies, half-begged, botched and deceived, opened-up and fragmented into the unforgiving loneliness of potato-ghosts, butt-ends of unlived life,—once he cried out he was *"a robot in a cave"* listening to the sound of a wave that kept breaking, slapping on a shore, that *"did not care"—etc.*)

The Twins did it! Sunk that Noah's Ark of numbers, broke the dreamwork . . . Imagine if someone else had done it! Slash and sparkle of blood, or your jaw broken by a perfectly timed express-train punch as you let your mouth go slack a second to accept the cigarette being offered. Extraordinary yellow eyes, very light and bright and odd. It's like landing two six-foot sharks in their blue and brown suits, in your living-room . . whenever they appear . . throw themselves forward like a rocket, propelled by a twist of the

whole muscular body. Chop-sock, gun, and knife. *The Twins* have
done some things. They frightened me . . . never "Piss-stick" though,
as they called him . . . "One great crazy guy" (who gave them winners).

. . . He *is* crazy: he should go through the door first; betting on
horses is "the greatest and most wonderful thing in the world";
Hump and I, *The Twins*, The Human Toilet, Les, and Nemone
Lethbridge the jockey, the German girl and Mrs. Lulka—all his
followers, his only friends are—: "*Cannibals laughing at an infant
king*"—and each time he wins he has "committed a glorious act with-
out precedent in the universal history of all time." Modest, too. —But,
it's those *technicals*, the only thing in the world which can really
scramble his brains! A thing P. has seen with the mouth of the heart
or eye of the soul, or whatever other organ he does it with—a horse
has come crashing right off the page, or through some other clue,
into this little pocket of sugar-candy we call the present from the
future to tell P. its intentions of winning,—or rather, *his* intentions
(*it* has already won, of course)—and then after a half-ton of huge
animal flesh with a little puppet curled up on top in the classic
womb-position, holding its own strings slack or tight, going around
quick curves in that moving forest of angry muscle on those knotted
pipe-stem legs at 40 m. per hr., and on and on its goes and wins!—
and *then* it's nothing, because in an excess of liberated energy the
horse has drifted out, swerved a little in front of some slow old
thing in lead socks bothering the leaders without a chance of win-
ning, who stumbles in his gait—"*objection*"—the red light goes on
on the great board, and the voice bawls out in a kind of obsequious
condescension that "the judges will examine the photograph before
the results of the race are official"—and then Chief Steward Keene
Dangerfield "sustains the objection" and the thing that has hap-
pened as foretold, the pure event, is not the result! Curdles my
mind, but what does it do to P.? Like last year, GOLDEN CALF
spooked by his own shadow burning down the stretch, infiltrated
his flight-line in front of KETTLE OF FISH, that tired old trooper
swishing around the lead with all his customary cheap speed in the
middle of a race, would have quit soon anyway, forced to suddenly
slow down, wobbles up the track pooped dead last . . . And mean-
while GOLDEN CALF is flying, crosses the finish line with all the
dangerous grandeur and sheer grace of reality, setting a new track
record for the mile and a sixteenth, 1:45 3/5 (would have paid too,

at least $22). But was taken down, disqualified. Zero, zip, zilch. O,
P. looked bad! Dream-bedaubed corpseskin. *"Rules is rules,"* Humpy
says: "When you're pushing your perambulator down the seven-lane
highway of life, not even a Mercedes-Benz can cut in front of you,
and get away with it!" Postic's ass is sucking air, slaps Humpy on his
namesake crony cruelly—: "Can't you talk about anything but cars?"
"Sure," the Hump is cute and ready, where did he get this?—*"A
yacht may luff as she pleases to prevent passing to winward—"*—
SWACK—*"I mean wind*ward*, but must never bear away to prevent
another passing to leeward—the lee side to be considered that on
which the leading yacht of the race carries her main boom."*

SWACK. Postic's punching his main boom into the wall. Knuckles
looked half-way up to the wrist. Lumps. It took both *Twins* to stop
him. Must have hurt like a son-of-a-bitch. But, all he talked about at
the hospital was Dangerfield and Judge Silvertooth, in the big black
box on stilts above the mirror and line and target at the end where the
camera lies hidden in its slot, taking the picture that forms and
holds the instant that is our forever . . . —I'm going on about him . . .
And all that bright garb! A kind of hokum to steel the nerves. Head-
dress, shoes, shirt, feather, etc., buckskins, beaded knife-sheaths,
feathers, hair-piece necklaces, seven pipes in the back of his belt,
and what not. But, it seems we are about to lose our lovely leathery
old Indian maiden Pocahontas Postic, whenever it speaks to him—
the feather. *The feather! . . .*

I forgot, it's falling. As he sings his ditty in a drunken, mortal cry:
*Gambling away the golden hours I worked so hard to hold—give me
more, O give me more—God make me bold!* The feather stands up
aslant in two letters, like black characters marching out of a white
infinity about to burn, spelling a name: SILVER SHIP. That was
the one!

THREE

THE CHILDREN

With white, silence-detonating faces—
And an inaccessible spark races
Free from, or trembles gently in each eye,
As they surround the old man. Now a cry
That they will not, he will not pass!
Their voices sound like broken glass.

They want to master and humiliate
His humble, slow stick-walking fate.
They want to pitch about, put out his spark—
And lead him through in unsunny dark.
But, deep calls unto deep. Then the children,
Seeing green-eyed God in him leave the man.

(I mean, they mark him once with a chalk-stick,
Toss loose bombs of earth that miss, run quick.)

IN A GARDEN

The light plays out a long, leaping shine—
sways—blazing charnel looks from her eyes.

The man snarls at a copper twig flaring
flowers like arrows of bodiless shadow.

And bright-red things, coiling, dusty-green things,
grow near him—reflecting bright fear, vague rage

on his face. Although the eyes are weeping
(and have far points like light on sea like steel)

they stab out at her. *"Ah!"*—her quick-thrilled, tender cry.
Then floating the long white fingers up

to his face, petals closing on their own
mystery, muttering like far sea now,

(she wants and does not want to be cast up
on his shore: a desert, discovering

itself dreamily, gently, as she touches—) she
lifts a tiny silken wing, white and wet,

from his tears. Pointing it with great, proud tact—
and murmuring, all adoration: *"See . . . ?"*

He sees what he is wavering to know.
The true mastery of pain, withdraws.

She smiles, unfurling her arms—then, he shows
he has found her, they kiss—the petal falls.

LACHIMAN GURUNG, GURKA FROM NEPAL

Lachiman Gurung, Gurka from Nepal,
Shot a hundred-or-so men after his hand fell
From the torch-touch-blast of a grenade. He shot
Them for hours, and when the gun got too hot

For one hand to load and shoot—squatting, he
Cradled, set his big toe to triggering it.
The easiest thing about this man to see
Is that he doesn't boast of the spirit

Or fact of his deed, pain, or the medal
(His Victoria Cross). He *is* proud of a dream,
A returning dream with the men who fell
When he turned superhuman. In this death's dream

The toothless old grizzled man waves an arm,
The one he lost (later, cut off)—with warm-
Running blood still shining, the shape of a hand.
He greets them. "—Love, is what I feel then. Understand.

"I was not expecting anything, I
Was not brave, but when I saw my friends die,
And my hand die, I was very, O so quite
Very angry. *'Come and fight, come and fight.*

While I live, I will kill you!' So, then some
Japanese did. Now, they are my memories'
Proudest moment. —In my dream, in my home
Together we drink and sing like happy bees!"

In the newspaper, I read this. And there
Was a picture of him, too. He has a rare
Clear-eyed look I cannot give a name—
Like burning air, friendlier than a flame.

But an enemy too, is gathered there.
Locked into the dead-spot at the center
Of each eye, staring at miracle,
Surrounded by that sunny wishing-well—

Or so I imagine from far away;
Saying much more than a hero would say,
Or dream. His medal gave him drinking-money.
He drinks with the gods, and they drink blood and honey.

AMSTERDAM STREET SCENE, 1972

The cupid-faced hooligan standing on tip-
toe with his tin cup comes down

on the beat of the roar on the floor of glitter-
ing cement while turning the white wheel

of his music-trunk, clapping coins in the cup
(a gull banks invisible to the eye to avoid a wall).

And with strange, charming deadness
puppets moved by wires drawn through their foreheads

move around a frail keyboard of bones, surrounded by
emblems and treasures, impaled on spikes (a great beast branded by

a Scarlet Woman, candlesticks, whips, wands, skulls, chalices,
a fox with a bird on a billhook, the lid of a tomb

flying off) all done in fond, dreamy pastels.
(Light drifting down like a bright brass puff,

lands on the rim of a cup like a halo) but no one gives.
People huddle by in ones and twos, smiling.

And as (no one hears it, now) the music runs down,
the wheel stops with a glad, eager grunt—

locking the puppets into the very dumbness
of each last gesture—he smiles once fast at them,

eyes as clear gray as the invisible eyes of glass
he gets behind, driving off—into the city's secret heart.

THE MOUNTAINS IN HOLLAND

Are made up,
As all monstrously magical frustrations are.

And, therefore:
I see no reason to believe they do not exist.

FOR JULES LAFORGUE

The city's intricate puzzle darkened
Night after night. Your quiet room blackened.
With pens honorable as spears poetry
Sought out melodramas of vulgarity.

How could you see them so well, Jules—
The eunuch dandies, and the fools
Pretending to be lovers (whose Real
Was holding hands at a lull in the meal)?

Moon-blazened by morality and luck,
You made them space for a spirit—then struck
Mortality so deeply into them, that O,
Implacably was yielded you—a great Pierrot,
Dancing on the mirror of the world, so
Hard his brightness broke in a bloody glow!

"*HE*—BELONGED-TO . . . ?

But O, how he gloried that life, and lives,
were ours! No trivial litter to be swept
by time, wept or kept. Though she did things, things wrong.
White crisscross hands, stick-body and hat-hair,
no-colored eyes rained red half the time. She
smelled like some kind of fruit when near him . . .
devoted to my father. Devoted too,
to my father—I hated my mother! When,
she stood in blind, affronted dismay, or
scuttled like a frightened spinster before
a fascist thug as he came closer. But O,
won his heart back by swift, lucid phrases
when she played with those black-dressed men in that show.
(He sat like a post in a pit, and *ah*'d.)
Bewildered, political, easily friendly,
cordially appreciative—she ran them down—
told them her desperate privilege was pursuit
of shadows. Now, why did she say that? Ah,
I know—she was not a fit vehicle
for *conveying* shadows anywhere. Least
of all to Hell, where she told them they must go.
She went to Hell biting a black nub-headed
lush wet spine of a snake my father
pulled out of her until its silk gouged raw,
started to rip and strip away grey gums,
into the zinc half-moon tub below.
Her pink ice-teeth! Kind, animal eyes . . .
She got smaller than herself. Went away
In a cart (mine!) pulled by animals, bouncing
on her stomach. While red and black swords clanged clanged.
And, my father! I dreamt he was God, I
lost all hope. My own ghost met me, a girl . . .
she told me! About all the people that went
bouncing away on rolling animals
who went riding through the world in grandeur.

to the wilderness where the Skull King sat,
in a cottage with a (young) elephant
who told us when we arrived: *not to doubt
the tooth of time*. Flesh and blood in the shadows...
A sunny room—heavier than rock.
I was in a little starched white dress,
as if no more than twelve years old. But,
underneath wore only brief black panties,
plus a push-'em-up bra, my patent leather
shoes shone so much they showed his underparts:
shrivelled grey cement, docile-haired, eyed.
And the tentacle twisting out of his face
trumpeted, as he came closer, broke his knees
in that strange way they have, winged-eared—
a gentle, philosophical animal—
menacing *me*! Toys, rocking-horse, music-box...
I looked for you that day, and did not find you.
Daddy, I loved you, I love you. O, *shut up*—
you're a dead man. And then the whole visit
began to smell badly. Yes and, *umbrellas
of flesh and bone*—opening, closing—
in a rain of blood. Closing, crying! Kicks, screams.
Deplorable. Awful! Shoddy. Webs sweep on,
splash red about. Faces where beautiful things
had been. So much in the heart of nature now—
weakened, wounded, played-out—lost. And, she!
*Und dann und wann eine weisse elephant,
l'ombrellone dell' elefantino.* Oh then,
she climbed the Never-To-Be-Forgotten stones...
of yesterday, today, and tomorrow! *I.*"

IN HIGHGATE CEMETERY, LONDON

Now fewer mighty ones, and more of the many—
Into filthy, gluttonous ripped throats of earth.
Only the stones saying what they have devoured,
And stone angels silent souling the earth no gain.

Big head of Karl Marx glowers above crops of stones,
On a pedestal like a sandwich-board. Near,
"This is the grave of A. Comfort." Small comfort, that!
And on a flat book with one stone page turning,

Momentous rays, and the deeply cut-in stone
George Eliot . . . gold ants moving a golden mesh.
Pigeons cover another. Swords of sunlight break
Upon bedizened necks. White lids slurring

Their eyes shut, like tiny tombstones. The black disc
Of the sun is there, the one seen when the sun is stared
Into too long—thin, and opposite to all vows
Of fire—on a strange, familiar name. And stones, *bright*—

In an insane, compassionate smile; making
Survival conscience, but wanting to die . . . !

DREAM:

A cat on gold-glowing black coals,
Like an enormous untouched bud
In the wincing glare,—must breathe air like hot towels.
Every hair of the black and white coat
Turns to gold, but does not burn. Eye a seeing leaf,
Sees me, blinks—as if I were beyond belief.
Then shooting claws of fire shine it red.
The cat sits afloat there, safe and alone. And wills
Me to understand it catches, kills
Something weak like the fear-ball in my throat.

I saw it as a true, imperfect picture
Of the blurred nakedness passionate friends can offer.
Growing smaller, and the fire seemed to be far,
Pale and shiny as a scar, insane, particular...

TO A PAINTER

Where cement glittering like sea spanned
its stone arm across the river
you stood
behind the blank-backed square—arm rounded, hand
outreaching its grasp with brush and color.

We walked through all the colors you had seen,
we went inside the scene you painted. *"Our life—"*
she, I,
blindly agreed. A gull, flew—almost unseen.
Sober, solitary sounds of city-life.

As we came up the bridge you did not stop
looking at us with lost, good-crazed green eyes.
A streak
of red or a scar on your cheek. "Make-up
of the gods" she called it. We turned our eyes

walking faster, almost shying right
past you and the world we'd said was ours.
But, no—
both had to look. *"Oh!"*—I heard her fright,
whispered. "Rigid, distorted. It devours!"

I thought. Objects, without life—fight. No style.
The only attribute was space. But just
before
we had gone by, a little crooked smile
at the side of your eye. I knew I must

see: *a river going, through banks like shores.*

FOR A FRIEND WHO DRIVES TOO FAST

Mira Rafalowicz

Moving your tense expressiveness along,
Only things going by, express speed. Wrong—

The clouds do, by refusing that same world
(Of streets, stores, skeletons with flesh) you have hurled

Rocketing by you, by your feet and hands—
The clouds do, those white and wayward islands

Of delight. See their great shapes, slow as breath . . .
Go through the magic and the dread of death.

RIDDLE

What rips and claws
Through the night—
Adding everything,
Valuing nothing,
Changing something—
Bright bright bright—
Yellow-eyed, jaws
Still-silent-blazing—
Then amazing,
The crash and purr
After . . .

Violence,
Meaningless
When—
The clean, consecutive kiss
Of silence,
And forms are seen as their shadows—
Again—
After that light,
Eye-seeing night—
A cataclysmic close,
Like darkening of a thousand windows . . . ?

answer: *lightning*

BIG BOY

Stumbling down stone steps, stomping the snakes of loosened
    shoelaces,
Big Boy comes carrying a gun, looking for *Someone* . . . Races
Faceheads of flowers and shadow-broken grass until towering
    trees fall up past.
A mother's fearful cry—an uneasy truce of words, the father's
    —following fast.
She reaches, through deep green haze . . . adoring aghast. Wet-
    stuck leaves
And red marls under him. To be fallen and found, O it grieves

Big Boy, dangerous, with a gun! Fireface sun? No. The target is
    her face of snow.
Silently seeing his shots go, hitting the warm bell of her voice,
    that gives the glow
Back to his name. But her hands flying over him, dancing birds,
Are so close freely fast he cannot shoot—and wandering wondering
    at their words
He follows those golden wings—till one falls still on the sealed
    rubber snout of the gun.

Aware of *Crumbleface*—watching now. Everywhere, *Everyone!*

FOUR

SEASONS AND STARS

1

Round, revealed peaches blaze in their box.
Light receives soul, blinds your loving
And you will never know or remember.
In the mind, surprise is the star.

2

The nipples, pricks of chimneypots
Stacked against towering tenement-
Wall sky, where waves of hot smell rise—
Man's sadness—ridiculous, alone.

3

The red-haired angel is at the
Yew-tree, muttering adorations.
He, she, think it is their passion.
Snake glides. The haggard corn has died.

4

And there, a little rat. Near fast
Grey curbstone running flat and grey
As frightened squirrel. Red legs up
Stiff, taught a trick by death, to beg.

5

Metal coffin sailing through air,
Landed where DeFaca was weeding.
Giant puppet-legs poked out. In-
Tact. *Scream*. The plane crashed farther on.

6

Volleys of children drum across
The bridge, shout at the fat squirrels
In Shakespeare's Garden. The statue
Stares. They are growing great and good.

7

Pigeons litter the track. The train
Rattles through. At last one thinks, where
Did the pigeons go? Lid of light
On blue rails, wheels, shuddering blows ...

8

"The cannibals are coming, the
Cannibals are coming." Big, red.
Yes, the cannibals are coming.
In the jungle, blossoming sex.

9

A hill of water, like arrows
Of water strengthlessly flying.
Curve of some emotion. Love? Love
Running, with a roar like battle ...

10

There is something Promethean
About simplest, everyday gestures.
Old man. Feeding emerald-headed
Ducks. Cords stand up his neck, like smiles.

11

Shot in the garment-center,
Fleeing a troubled delicatessen—
Hid with a synod of bugbears—
Snooking them, eating chalazas.

12

There is in the bush of ghosts, a
Red River before *Lost-Gain-Land.*
Where, clothes off, you ride a stick, cross.
Things fight for your clothes, not your soul.

13

Cimon finally earned a wife,
Cutting her real husband in half.
But what are we to make of this?—
Mighty heart, manhood, love—now, all his.

14

When you imagine, it is there.
And then you are hearing to hear:
A sound like hysterical laughter—
Steep, empty sky-mirrors breaking!

15

"O, wow," she says when she sees swans.
And she still steals things out of stores.
In bed, a human radiator;—
Makes noise, gives heat, but—does not move.

16

A bisque of flotid, marmid stot,
Renned by—Words of savage spirits,
Who like to get it while it's hot,
The spoon nestling, dandling its—

17

In her heart, the little match-girl
Always knew she would survive. All
Cold, unkindness. Scratched on the void,
Of the city—*tiny tears flamed.*

18

The color of the soul is love.
More than mountainous, its tower.
Eyed, in the blood—things stir, break, speak.
The seasons turning into stars.

19

In such a summer, one could believe
The high avenues of trees held up
The tower, because they hid it.
A wrong she did, becoming leaved . . .

20

Basket of flowers overturned
In the park. Two girls lashing
Each other slowly, lovingly—
With their long black rivering hair.

21

The white-faced clock tick-tocked, tick-tocked.
An imaginary, secret heart;
Never known, or seen—animal, loud—
Whose face at evening comes for love?

22

Well into the rivers of color
Within her eye, the sunlight turned
A strange motion. Seen—fragile, as new
Grass—the moment of its white heart.

23

Old thin white woman hooded.
A bird with your brow, stands flapping.
O, disappointedly . . . And further,
That . . . figure of a black statue.

24

She is less seen than light around
Her clouds . . . Shooting terror and pride,
White, finally free—the death's head
Of infinity floats and smiles.

25

Flame-shaped puff of black cotton. Man
Made of red shadow. A cobra-
Necked bottle, with yellow nipple-top.
A gold whip. White pads. The red face.

26

These powdered and nacreous faces,
Asterisk-eyed, purse-mouthed,—bodies
Blown through our angry eyes like stained
Meat—must have our smiles, our darkness.

27

The sky is a low, heavy lid.
Bells battle, banners tremor. The dream
Dreams on,—of grief, and revenge—
Scratching, preening, grinning, posing.

28

But the tower shattered down, shat
Down, pieces of itself, slowly.
Pointing gun-wands, we searched. Nothing.
Ha-hah ha-hah, ha ha ha ha.

29

Castle of The Whispering Truth,
Has a Chapel Perilous, where
Lulu the Hermaphrodite shines. Pallid
Candles lengthen on brass sockets.

30

Ardvari, dwarf robbed of his gold
By Loki, consumed hate, clouted love,
Rinsed the ruck and rut of revenge—
By one bold look. She died laughing.

31

Gentle dined at the Inn last night,
And said meat was not a fit dish.
Then gave all there a terrible fright
By what he did to the fish.

32

He sees his children in the night,
Digging for the buried light,
In graves where randy demons play
And talk the psychiatric way.

33

"Snakes in the icebox, holes in the wall—
Snakes in the icebox, holes in the wall.
Snakes in the icebox—holes in the wall . . .
Ain't doin' me no good at all!"

34

A mermaid in a flying lake,
Forced a fortress. Towers tumbled
Into fish-soup. Wings of water
Carrying the whole thing. Know-how.

35

Perfumes of Carthage in her hair,
She might have died a slut unseen,
Except the cold and trembling air
Whitened her to a powdery queen.

36

WHOLE TOWN TURNS INTO A BROTHEL.
GIANT HITS FIVE-HUNDRED FOOT HOMER
IN PHOENIX. BOY DIES TWICE. STRANGLER
OF SEVEN REPENTS, IS LONELY.

37

Born among valences of corn,
A sleek black flower grew over
Shut stone wall, where golden crucifixes
Fell at night. Earth, into despair.

38

A lady leapt to her death through
Sunlit snow. Who knows why snow fell
By her like her pain—pain on which
The golden sun slept without strain?

39

O the summertime has come, and
The leaves are sweetly blooming,—and
The wild mountain thyme, all along
The blooming heather . . . Will ye go?

40

I will build my love a tower,
By yon clear crystal fountain. And
There I will pile all the flowers
Of the mountain. Will ye go?

41

"I gave all I own, gave all . . . Air
Through the cypresses, so softly,
But winds from the wall . . . strange. Bodies,
Holding like hands, fingers let fall."

42

The towering green torches: *trees*.
The fabulous ruin of Autumn.
Becoming bare, the brown bodies.
Then stilled green eyes, see wild whiteness.